SPLITTING
MOC

SPLITTING THE
MOON

A COLLECTION OF ISLAMIC POETRY

JOEL HAYWARD

KUBE
PUBLISHING

First published in England by Kube Publishing Ltd,
Markfield Conference Centre
Ratby Lane, Markfield,
Leicestershire LE67 9SY
United Kingdom
Tel: +44 (0) 1530 249230
Fax: +44 (0) 1530 249656
Website: www.kubepublishing.com
Email: info@kubepublishing.com

The right of Joel Hayward to be identified as the author of this
work has been asserted by him in accordance with the Copyright,
Designs and Patents Act, 1988.

A Cataloguing-in-Publication data record is available from the
British Library.

ISBN 978-1-84774-034-2 *paperback*

Cover Design: Inspiral Design
Typesetting: Nasir Cadir

Dedication

I wrote these poems as an offering of profound thanks to my Creator with a hope that insha'Allah the poems will also bring pleasure to other readers and repay the unfailing patience and love I have received from my wonderful and beloved family.

Deus est regit qui omnia

Contents

Preface

From the very day on which I excitedly spoke my testimony of faith *(shahadah)* in a Peterborough mosque in parrot-fashioned Arabic – interestingly, as the only Caucasian amongst hundreds of happy and congratulatory Asians – I have been recording my spiritual journey not only in various articles for magazines and newspapers, but also in poems that I use, most days, as my primary means of examining, making sense of and expressing my thoughts, feelings and experiences.

My own voyage into Islam commenced on that worst of days: 11th September 2001. I was already a well-established defence scholar when 9/11 occurred and I could immediately see through the mistaken claim by several governments and the media that the world had changed because of a dangerous new phenomenon which was supposedly widespread within Islam: militant radicalisation. Unlike many people who seemed unable to find alternative explanations, I knew from my own extensive travels in Islamic lands and from research and reading that the great faith of Islam was no more violent than the faith I had practised for decades: Christianity. Indeed, I knew then Osama bin Laden was no more representative of Islam than Oklahoma City bomber Timothy McVeigh was of Christianity.

The events of 9/11 nonetheless had a profound impact on me. I felt increasingly troubled by a growing public misperception that, while not all Muslims were terrorists, all terrorists were Muslims. Some of my own friends and family members, and even my students, talked negatively about Islam and seemed certain that the terrorists' motivations must have originated from within the Qur'an.

Up until 9/11 the Qur'an had meant little to me. In our garage while growing up we had a tatty set of old green books, the 51-volume set of Harvard Classics, which supposedly contained xii ● Splitting the Moon: A Collection of Islamic Poetry

humankind's most important works of literature and philosophy. The books had belonged to my grandad but faded and grew grubby in our spiderweb-filled garage. I was (and am) a veracious reader and occasionally I would dust off one of those volumes and read it. In a volume titled *Sacred Writings*, I read as a ten-year-old boy a strange set of words that I didn't understand: "Mohammedan: Chapters from the Koran". I glanced through this fascinating material, which reminded me of *The Thousand and One Nights*, which I'd recently enjoyed, but for no real reason I chose instead to take Homer's *The Odyssey* inside from the garage to read in bed. That epic poem filled me with love for the ancient world and eventually led me to learn Greek and undertake undergraduate and honours degrees in Classical Studies. I have often wondered how my life might have been different if, as a boy, I had devoured the Qur'an instead of Homer's masterpiece. But, as I have since learned, Allah knows best.

I never actually got around to reading the Qur'an before 9/11. I studied the Bible intensely (even learning Hebrew to read it in its original tongue) and I read it many times as I tried to make sense of both Judaism (the religion of some of my mum's forebears) and Christianity, which I embraced as a young man. Yet the Qur'an remained a mystery until 2001.

Concerned by the events of 9/11, I decided to study the Qur'an in search of anything that might have inspired such wanton violence against innocent people. I started at the beginning and read slowly and carefully through to the end, all the while making notes on verses that might support the violent and aggressive philosophy and actions of the 9/11 terrorists. I found some verses that dealt with armed combat within wars of justice, but none that would support indiscriminate or disproportionate violence during those wars, and none that would support *any* violence outside of formal warfare.

What I did find in the Qur'an shocked me to my core. Within the Qur'an I found the same prophets as those revealed within the Bible I had enthusiastically studied. I found Adam, Noah, Abraham, Moses and other biblical prophets. More importantly, in the Qur'an I also found my own favourite: Jesus the son of Mary. As a Christian I had always revered Jesus, but I had never known that the Qur'an spoke of Jesus in precisely the same way that I had come to see him: as a wonderful, righteous messenger who brought glad tidings and warnings to the children of Israel.

That does not mean that I had ever found the religion of Christianity entirely fulfilling. From the moment when I first felt the call of God as a young man I had always believed that God was truly the master of the universe and the creator of everything within it. He was Sovereign, All-powerful and All-knowing. I accepted that fully and willingly. Yet I had a problem. The Christian teaching of the Trinity – the Church's insistence that the one God was actually three in one, and that Jesus was himself God and one third of the so-called Godhead – sat uncomfortably with both my intellect and my heart. I could not rationally see logic in it and I could not embrace it emotionally. Initially I wanted to believe what the Church taught. Surely two billion Christians could not be wrong about something so important. This issue mattered to me. It bothered me. After all, the Book of Deuteronomy (6:4) had proclaimed: "Hear, Oh Israel, the Lord our God the Lord is One." This revelation to Moses sits so centrally within both Judaism and Christianity that I found its power inescapable. I also knew that Jesus felt likewise about that specific revelation. When asked by a scribe what he considered the most important of God's commandments, the Book of Mark (12:29) quotes Jesus as replying: "The first of all the Commandments is, Hear, Oh Israel, the Lord our God the Lord is One."

When I first read the Qur'an systematically after 9/11 I was amazed by the compatibility between the Qur'anic revelation and my beliefs as a non-Trinitarian monotheist. I was especially impressed by the Qur'anic emphasis on the messages revealed through Abraham, Moses and Jesus; messages I had believed for decades. On the other hand, I knew nothing about the Prophet Muhammad and the message that he seemed to bring to the Arabs. I began to read and study with the aim of learning whether Muhammad revealed anything new, whether the emphasis of this revelation was consistent with or different to those of previous prophets, and whether Muhammad himself lived a life, as Jesus had, worthy of emulation.

The eventual conclusion I reached after years of intellectual enquiry through in-depth study was life-changing. After methodically reading the Qur'an twenty times in seven years I accepted that God's revelation through Muhammad was identical in every way to that revealed through former prophets. God is one! His oneness cannot be divided! He is worthy of all praise and He asks us to enjoy lives of willing submission. Moreover, unlike previous prophets, Muhammad – absolutely worthy of emulation – revealed a calling not just to the children of Israel, and not just to the Arabs (as I had initially thought), but to all of humanity.

What was I to make of my inescapable intellectual conclusion that the Qur'anic revelation was logical, coherent, consistent and persuasive, especially as I then had no emotional desire to embrace a "different" religion? The answer is easy for me to give. I submitted. On the basis of my rational investigation, I decided to take a step of faith knowing that my heart would probably quickly catch up with my head. I chose to become a Muslim. My heart has since caught up and now both mind and heart are in unison.

Throughout my years of spiritual exploration I continued to write poetry, much of it dealing with these very issues, but also, of course, with everything else I experienced or observed. Throughout creatively fertile periods I wrote one or two poems every day, while during barren phases I wrote far fewer, sometimes only one per week. My eventual conversion – which occurred after I saw four or five hundred Indonesian shoppers praying their *Zuhr* prayer together in a Jakarta convention centre and *I knew* I ought to be kneeling with them – ushered in a fertile period that has, thank

God, remained right up until the time of finishing this book. Hundreds of poems have arisen from within me: most in praise of Allah but many also to capture moments of curiosity, wonder, joy, frustration, and disappointment at things I have observed occurring within or affecting the surprisingly disunited *ummah*.

In many ways I became a Muslim at an unusual and difficult time, with relations between Muslims and non-Muslims severely strained by various factors. These include 9/11, the so-called War on Terror, 7/7 and other bombings, bans in European countries of minarets and burkas, Qur'an burnings, the rise of anti-Islamic groups like the English Defence League (the loutish and hateful protests of which I have twice observed first-hand) and a flood of new books which erroneously condemn Islam as brutish and backward. I have experienced anti-Muslim hostility myself, including a savage and highly dishonest tabloid attack and a steady trickle of unpleasant emails from anonymous people who claim I have betrayed my western values, and rendered myself unfit to hold senior posts, by embracing Islam. Some of the poems in this collection respond to those foolish and unenlightened views.

As a poet my changes of religious affiliation and outlook could not have occurred at a more exciting time. Everything *seems* intense; everything *feels* intense. I therefore thank Almighty God that he let me come to Islam after having observed it from outside for four decades and then, in an era bursting with dramatic things to write about, he opened my eyes to the majesty of the Qur'anic revelation. I am a very fortunate poet and I pray insha'Allah that my poems have captured at least some of the colour, verve and pathos of today's Islamic world.

Joel Hayward
September 2011

Beyond

I wanted to write a poem
Of You
That does not
Include me
But my first word here was
I and I
Want to say I'm sorry
But that's also about me

You Oh Lord
Are beyond words
Anyway
Even the prettiest
Are shabby
Compared to Your heart
Of love

Even words that sound
The same
As their meaning –
Scrumptious, Graceful
Sweetheart –
Are clumsy and ugly
Compared to
Your name

Words as fragrant
As their flowers –
Carnations, violets,
Goldenrods,
Dahlias –
Wither as weeds
When Your warmth
Radiates as midday
From the pages of Your Book

A poem of You
Needs only one word
Or ninety-nine
And it is finished

The Voyage of a Scholar

On the day that paper clips and files
And memos snowed upon a city
I opened an unfamiliar book
To see what had brought that storm

Each night I brushed back dreams
By turning pages of profundity
To learn what had placed death
In the eyes of passport photos

The heavens opened for
Forty days within my mind and
Soul in a Noah's flood of
Confusing certainties

The willing dead were absent in
Every word but my forty days
Left greater questions buoyant
And curiosity unvanquished

I sailed twenty times
In seven years through
Surah seas of calm swells
Pushed by winds of conscience

Twenty times I charted their
Depths – truly Pacific –
Before I knew that I
Knew nothing

When tranquil winds lifted
La ilaha illallah I heard a soft
Muhammadur Rasulullah
Slip without thought from my lips

A book read twenty times asked
When I would embrace its truth
And in a small stillness I replied
Now oh Lord, Now

Arab Spring

Hands clenched, passions wrenched
Hearts ablaze, these days of rage
Shouts in the air, pauses for prayer
Streets, squares, mosques, theirs

Hearts freed, knees bleed,
Proud, aloud, unbowed crowd
Freedom sought, its shape unthought
Unknown ideal, substance not real
Grass is greener, democracy leaner

Cigarette smoking, despots choking
Forgotten youth and unseen truth
Confused eyes, fleeing spies, sons' lies
Streets, squares, no longer theirs

Ranting, railing, panting, flailing
Heads full of pain, nothing to gain
Power grasping, compromise asking
Opportunity lost, everything cost
Posterity crushing and the end fast rushing

Your Book

I read your words and hear whispered reminders
As my tired eyes struggle across dots and black curves
While I ponder and wonder and stare holding my chin
As wisdom tries to sneak inside crowds of thoughts on life

I read your words and hear my slow breathing, deep
And know that on that day it will cease and I'll sleep
And then blink inside your sun-drenched calmness
As I step forward to hear your thoughts on my life

I read your words and feel the tug of sad conscience
And know whom I've let down, helped and annoyed
When you wanted more and yet I gave so little
And wasted time as I walked too quickly through life

I closed my eyes darkly and called back your words
And slid them silently from my tongue into my room
Where they'll circle and swarm close to my pillow
As I ask for their meaning and the warmth of their life

I spoke your words quietly to friends and strangers
With the force of a hurricane, unnoticed, so soft
While I knew that the wind would tug later at thoughts
And poke hearts with gentle fingers on the hand of life

All in All

Great whales' hearts thud
Allah ... Allah
Eight times
Each grey
Minute

The hummingbird calls
Faster, much faster
The name in
A whir of
Acclamation

Knuckly stiff fingers
Count misbahah beads
In resin while
The mind strokes
Each for a second

A baby's colic cry
And a mother's
Soft shushing
Hold a meaning
Understood

The aches of the
Lonely and penitent
Are never felt
By only
One

In everything lives
The memory of
An echo of that
First word
"Be"

Florida Pastor

Tool, cruel, mistaken fool, grabs for fame, causes shame
Christ would cringe, this done in his name
Flames winning, Shaytan grinning, charred mess, success
Promise spoken, entirely broken, failed a single test
Eyes blind, blackened mind, should've read the book
A tiny pyre, the world's ire, three minutes all that it took
Wanted, gained, anger blamed on Muslims always hated
Love missing, wisdom dismissing, happy with Muslims baited

Anger unbound, fists pound, Shaytan fanning the flames
Control left behind, grief in mind, anger pulsing in veins
Streets swollen, crowds emboldened, victims caught in rage
The irony is, the book forbids this, hatred not on a page
Message ignored, calmness abhorred, playing into his hands
World worse for that man's curse, tension sadly expands
One copy alight, one billion alright, their power even greater
God's mighty word, always heard, untouched by one Muslim hater

Prayer in Peterborough

Long John Silver
With eyes aged like stars
In my mosque, on a crutch

Subhana Rabbi al-A'la
I whisper past bent knees

He has one and sits in God's sight
On a chair wearing purity
And whispers too and smiles
Not at me or others but at the One
Who took his leg and gave him a prop

Bright-eyed adventurer watching
The horizon searching for land
Where rivers flow beneath
And upon its white shore of sand
He'll leave footprints as he strides

Long John Silver
With diamonds that see
In my mosque, on a crutch

Rabbana Lak al-Hamd
He responds in a mind full of gold

Beneath God's words in a dome
While light stretches to reach his cheek
And strokes it with a mother's love
As I echo three words and smile
Not at him or others but at the One
Who gave him more than he lost

White haired voyager gazing eyes closed
A journey stopping without ending
When he sinks upon young knees
And scoops living water from the source

Thank You

Eyes squinted at the sun for the merest moment
It remained emblazoned inside closed lids
For longer than the squint then faded
When I turned away

Prayers climbed to You from a plaintive heart
You Oh Allah shone down upon me brighter
Radiance greater and without fading
When I rose from my knees

Eyes without a blink gazed up at a cool moon
My thoughts rose and brushed its ice-white face
And You Oh Allah returned warm answers
When I asked what all things mean

Anxieties sailed out beyond the ocean's only line
You Oh Allah raised a breeze to fill the sails
And You sent me comfort on lapping waves
Whenever life caused deeper footprints

That City That Day

I saw fear in Leicester
Sons and fathers whispering
Sentries standing guard
Mosques and shops
Empty inside crowded outside

I saw suspicion in Leicester
Waiting eyes watching
Looking for the arrival
Sighing with resignation
Minds chanting prayers

I saw calmness in Leicester
Brothers as bars on a steel rail
Older steadying younger
Wisdom with beards
Jaws clenched and no fists

I saw democracy in Leicester
Permissiveness in uniform
Reluctant toleration
Authority manifest
Allowing to limits but not beyond

I saw hatred in Leicester
Empty eyes and open mouths
Knuckles and noise in grunts
Herded and cornered and held
Braying and jubilant in losing

I saw Old England in Leicester
The red and white of the nation
Their hollow emptiness
Protest and pride without point
The English Defence League

I drove home from Leicester
Weighing so much more
Mind's eyes staring at stupidity
Memory blocking strangers' curses
To hear the quietness of brothers

The Six at Thawr

The first said Oh Allah
My labour is for You
You honour me
You ask me to weave
Silken concealment
Silver sun-gleaming
Eight working together
Let it please You
You chose a dot a spot
And not an armour-clad army

The lovers said Oh Allah
We create life for you
Encased white in ovals
In a hand-shaped house
Twigs knitted within clefts
He said I brought them
She, I plaited them
Let our love please You
You chose two small who coo
And not a shield wall of angels

The fourth said Oh Allah
Let not our cleft shadow
Form an unwanted tomb
Deafen the ears of hate
To my frozen breath
Or gulping swallow
Send us an army of angels
To defend the Wise
And let me join them
With courage in Your service

The fifth said Oh Allah
You fill our cave of two
And are the third
Soothe my beloved
Who first said yes
Touch him with calm
They are deaf who listen
And blind who watch
There is no work for warriors
We need no angels
You are All

Wounded at Uhud

That scar red-iron-seared to seal and heal
Lip face and pride torn ripped split by a rock
A random pick in a war of shouts and sand
To fit the hand of the blind in mind who bent
Wanting hate sent to that leader then bleeder

It rests still mean unseen by eyes except God's
Who reclaimed the red that stained it a while
That plunging meteor of shame gravity-called
Guided by the hisser from a strong arm of hate
It knocked the Great from his feet in Arabian heat
To earth flat with a groan clothed heavy in mail
Circles linked as if sewn shielding the worthy

Above the Great a friend lay cushion-pinned
To save the Chosen and a better place win
The Prophet's death filled the sky shouted high
Turned the foe's slaying to braying and staying
And a sigh-yawning mouth of fleeting time
A moment teeth broken to rise from sore dirt
Falling from ringed shirt with surprise as he climbed
The hill of confusion which rang with the gloating
Of claims that the future was shaken then slain

Yet the Prophet knew through the dust of a daze
That truth dawning would blaze justice one day
When the living scarred smile that they saw
Proclaimed God was a shield sword and more

Transfixed

Such beauty so close
Fluttered and
Fascinated

A butterfly
Impossible to catch
Yet if Allah willed
She would alight
Upon his arm

If Allah willed

For what should he pray?

The Calling of Moses

Shade-searching exile alone thronged by thoughts
Deep as a well while the sheep lost and found
Lapped at a sparkle on the ground's burned crust
Leather unstrapped so that his dust-covered feet
Could holy ground meet as miracles danced
On each fingering branch untouched by the heat
That crackled in flames beneath the mile-wide wrist
Of an arid rock fist holding wild emptiness

Then the growling roar of a whispered caress
Said Go with your heart like the tree's radiant glow
Show with lustrous right hand and a staff slithering
That the kohl-eyed scarab king who sin-hiding
Smears sun-frightened arms with animal fat and
Rests with fears sat on the footstool of slaves
Must now use his ankh to unlock as a key
Those who loved Allah and sought to be saved

True Wealth

Oh Great Lord grant me treasure
I pray insha'Allah for a parchment
Unrolled lambskin tattered and dull
Inked now faintly with an island unknown
A map of a far-flung forgotten speck
A fleck of sand on a blue glass floor
I know the mark to find: the X

Oh I will risk and struggle and hunger
To reach that lost and empty atoll
The lure of that wealth enticing me
I will pace the ground counting steps
Chest tight and mind full and swollen
With a craving for what I'll have to dig
To reach deep where it lies in ancient clay
In an arched chest held tight by rust
And a lock forgotten by its long-lost key

Oh Great Lord end my years of poverty
I pray insha'Allah for a transformed life
Enriched by the contents of that box
Make me wealthy with its glinting bounty
I feel greedy for it but want to share
Let me spread fortune to those like me
Who have seldom held a single piece

Give my arms strength sufficient
To lever ajar that unearthed casket
To plunge my fingers into the wealth
That I crave and You hid but let me find
Through driving desire and a brow of sweat
A strongbox full only of my heart's desire:
Not coins or jewels or gold or silver but
Wisdom wisdom wisdom wisdom

Today's World

What will you think when you learn
That I have been bowing low like
Those who pulled down the brothers?

What will you think when you learn
That with hands by ears each day
I whisper the phrase of the cockpit?

What will you think when you learn
That I discover truth in the book
Found in lost luggage?

What will you think when you learn
That I have chosen the same faith
As the one in the cave?

How will you know
That I would never let my elbows
Touch theirs on the floor?

How will you know
That I have reclaimed the words
Stolen by the devil in the pilot seat?

How will you know
That I read the same book
But cannot see the same words?

How will you know
That I would not share his path
Or enter the wasted air of his cave?

You Know My Life

My petrol tank's half empty
I know it and keep looking

Monitoring the gauge
Often, aware, acutely

Snaking roads winding
Crawling mountain passes

Straining, that noisiest gear
First, revving, pulling, working

Often lost and u-turning
Detours annoying, consuming
Too many times, with time wasted

My satnav in glovebox sits
But used? Seldom bothered,
Knew better (that's me, though)

You had pumped my fuel: full!
You were clear with directions

Gave me your satnav, that gift
A map of roads, a great book

You watch me driving (too slowly?)
To your chosen location

Knowing what I don't and find
Anxiety-aching, vehicle ageing:

When my tank will run dry
And my engine will die

Ironies

You ride on a train
And create sideways glances

In a beard they see an outsider

Dark

I pray in a mosque
Full of sideways glances

In a shaven jaw they see an outsider

Fair

Nothing to fear?

Bit unfair?

I think of the Prophet

A little oil in the lamp
Bronze, Aladdinesque
Light wisps and whispers
As it swims from its prison
Up golden blue an inch rich
And blinks and shrinks the room
Creates a curved darkness
That hides walls upon which
Your words hang on nails
In letters I cannot read
At least not well enough yet
Still better than He
Who recited in shakes
When lampless light spoke

And broke solitude's hold
And said that the Almighty
Had a goal a role for that great soul
To breathe truth upon those
Who had blocked their ears
Walked astray without fears
And the cave world-sized small
The heart bigger still the birth
Of the mankind-wide call to
Forget wealth self and to bow
Face paper-flat down and in awe
On the floor while the soul will
To Him soar with adoration full

Not for Himself

Blistering chipped woodworker's fingers
Grip a chisel while his mallet-tapping
Heart pushes spirit-filled meek purity
Through stretched veins work-swollen
And raised on skin which the sun esteems
With glistening sweat salt-silver drops and
He grips God's Musa-bellowed words
Far tighter and with eyes of sad happiness
Welcoming the God-gratitude of the
Poor and poorly, guileless and guilty

Sweet steel words highly honed
Slide from his lips between prayers to
Sharply shave away seven peeling slivers
From the worm-rotten wood of a Deen
Stolen, ruined and chewed for so long
By those spitting out God's truth
Bitter to their tasteless tongues

Others – the faithful few true –
Saw the builder's blunt words
As a sword whetstone-sharpened
Along edges twinned to the point and
High swung sun-lustrous in battle
Against the hiss-whisperers who lingered
Hidden in shadows behind those doors
Which open from thoughts unto words

Thus trust in the One swelled in the few
Whose ears heard "of Him" never "of Me"
Over and always the message no other
From the one working wood with miracles
And knuckle-cut bleeding and weeping
The fasting praying whip-wielding man
Who kicked over tables enmity-making
And said with heart, mind, soul and strength
Love the Lord your God with all those and more

Chosen One

You never felt snow tighten your skin with a sting
You never searched for the shore from the crest of a wave
You never grinned at the gait of a penguin
You never saw a whale's grey fluke sink after rising
You never breathed in coffee's warm rich aroma
You never heard the clearing of a smoker's throat
You never saw headlights peer through dawn fog
You never smiled at an American accent
You never waited in a queue at the bank
You never cringed at the words of a driving instructor
You never sat and failed a biology test
You never kicked a football across the road
You never changed batteries in a tv remote
You never emptied a lawn-mower's grasscatcher
You never rushed to catch a bus then missed it

Yet exulted He chose you
Praise and glory to Him
Picked you from this world
And for it
The last in the line
The path straight to follow
To Him high above all
Alhamdulillah!

114 Surahs

Whispered surahs sneak
delicately hushed
as elderly dreams
under doors
and swathe his face
in shading cool
like the old one's
muslin shroud
before curling swirling
turning burning
into a reluctantly
frail trail yearning of
smoke from the conscience
and slipping
seeping easing –
while he watches
with eyes sighs cries –
into his mind
as a whispering
teasing friend
who finger taps
songs of change
love and submission
inside his domed bone
while kissing his eyes

crushing his heart
with a tender clench
to make him groan moan
want not nonchalant
his life's great reward

Splitting the Moon

Quraysh greybeards greysouls
Heartspots black enlarging
Ears not hearing sired confessions
Jealous eyes clouding the moonsplit
Here there in the early dark low
Trickery – bitter thoughts reason – jealous
As the mummy-king was at Musa's snakestick

"Behold" said the one knowing
That the open-handed offering –
Glad tidings, warnings, al-Furqan –
Would split the worlds of which One ruled
Like Isa's sword of mysterious portent
While the greybeards' necks craned
Disbelief reined, Greatsoul's heart pained

Shamed later seeing and knowing
Greysouls scorched yet forgiven
Remembered the whitelight as two
Their mocking over but trickling regret
Their unseen great son whispering
Grace undeserved, the smile unreserved
All knees agreed beneath radiance untorn

Knees of the Revert

Nose, eyebrows, breath on woven warmth
Weight on wrists and not in heart

Eyes sensing lids black with glowing focus
Thoughts emptying, spilling purer and
Matching wet arms, ankles, washed
With mumbled clarity in rhymes
Pushed from lips that love and want
Closer closeness than the vein of thoughts

The Creator seeing spine, shoulders, soul
Then palms on knees, chin on chest

The Creation feeling aching inexperience
Not sat thus since the days of chalk
When the Lover of Innocence touched
The imagination greenwood growing with
Castles, cowboys, kings and then whispered
Don't stop hearing as years grab tight

With words forgotten age brings pain
Feet tucked and knees stretched
The ache of joints and remembered sins
Allahu Akbar freedom gained from
Pressed low face and plaintive heart
Repentant prayer and Great Lord here

The Islamic Bookshop in Leicester

It's bodyheat close, rackety, heavenish
below constricted tower walls of words
and covers like Yusuf's garment and titles
that make this contented neck screw to read
vertically, eyes scanning down-up on sides
like a tesco barcode reader beep-free
except inside this mind when, ding,
that's one he needs ... well, wants ... no, needs

Muhammad, history, Qur'an, meaning, yes
the shelves, section, corner, row, world
and everything with nothing else than this
man's mindhunger, with eyes enlarging and soul
grocery shopping, wallet ready to shrink and
teeth clutching knowledge that grows so easily

They squeeze past often, salaming, aware
of skin and chin unlike yet like and his
purpose, focus, mission, sensing, seeing, and
they catch questions, weighing tons, nothing
light but they answer in ounces, a diet
of expectations while he needs to gorge

They watch from eyes aside his
ascent to laddery Everest's summit
not to miss – he thinks – what
ceiling, height concealing, might
have there: an answer, a question,
a bearhug of ideas and fresh ambitions and
the joy of the thump of new uncertainty

Ohhhhh to know all, more too, and, in the blink
of the bathplug swirl of knowledge, wisdom gets
sucked as a blackhole and pulled into that
mind that needs ... well, wants ... no, needs
to serve the One who said Be and he was
while the clock gallops to win its race and then
to ask him to salute the One who owns That Day

Lord of the Worlds

I swallow time
in swigs
and think of You
I blink blue, sore
and see forever
but in shards
with thick-skinned coffee
while oft-thumbed diary
pages within this mind
slide, thrice
over palms and feet

I feel time touch
yet suffer sneers
and claws that etch my face
as a postman's
while You tumble through
and share
apple-breath breezes
with children old and new

You kept my trophy
safe and somewhere
aglow with lustre
while I walked on water
and sank
within friends' laughter
as You kept a garden
and plucked hope and purpose
to sate our weak

Voices in the hallway
murmur He is One
through a door of lacy
black widows' spinning
and this heart races
to drum a cadence
in concrete as a dance

Tip a cathedral downside up
and watch priests' gowns
fall over surprise
as an owl flies in day's gold
and stares into waters
rippling with an unseen splash
spreading from Your hand extended

Iman

I filled my heart to overflowing
It spilled and pooled without me knowing

Regret upon awareness grew
With hope that rug can stay as new

This mad recluse's clumsy hands
Delight at prayer mat's soothing strands

What You Do

I flew a kite with a key
so You could light the sky
and flick a bounding bolt
towards my darkened home

You drew a storm from the sea
and rattled window panes
with gusts of supremacy that flung
my back door from its jam

Spiralling allure stings these eyes
which watch through squints while
tempests tear comfort from my chair
and crack my mirror into slivers

Master and Servant

He smiled and he burned
and died and lived
immediately
and gasped and grasped
and loved
impassionedly

He laughed and he knew
and spoke and choked
impulsively
and rejoiced with no voice
and loved
compulsively

He touched and he soared
and grew and flew
exultantly
and raced to embrace
and loved emphatically

Her Journal

Through her summer dress
sunrays warm her

Between cloud gaps only

She picks three fragile blue flowers
from her wildweed garden
to dry – in flat foreverness –
between the pages of the journal
that only she and her Creator know she keeps

Her pages hold truth: the oily transparent petal stains
from tears that slipped from her cheeks
onto her delicate creations before the pages closed

Faizan-e-Madina Mosque

Italian boots point among trainers sandals scattered
Socks cat-pawing spongewalk on carpets peaceful
Brown, black, blue soul-windows open
Casting light white from other to each
Curiosity satisfaction no suspicion
Shoulders together not soldiers ever
Wars unwanted save self, sin, him
White amidst not, colourless, covered and copying
Noses foreheads submission breathing pressing

Cube black facing consciences confessing
Oneness greatness Allah

The Certainty of Not Knowing

I die more each day and no-one notices but You
And those who find me in print from time to time
Those close see the same except for hair length
Or a pound or two or tiredness and shadows
Yet its truth sighs in the mirror though it has no feel
As it comes at night when I cannot care

I die more each day and no-one causes it but You
Though You let me quicken or slow it with choices
That You know I'll make and which I call freedom
Or foolishness or wisdom or experience
And I don't know which pulls the end nearer
Or keeps it unknown as a distant dark horizon

I live more each day as you prepare me for You
And flick away specks and teach me to sweep
With a broom made from pain, Astagfirullah
And I don't want those I love to hear words
That could forever sound louder as a legacy
Than the soft and wise when I leave for home

I live more each day as I gather truths from You
Walking the path You waited for me to reach
After so long in shoes too big yet so tight
With my eyes down in books without pages
While You held out one with orchestral words
That now play warmly as I hope for sunrise

The Office

My car windscreen grill too full of nature
Collects blossoms pink from a shadowless tree
The shortest of brothers shoulder to shoulder
Where I park in the morning and prepare
For my day with unspoken prayer and a glance
In the mirror from which deep blue and gold
Hangs a pendant with two names in glass
Yours and his and a blizzard-blue tassel
Almighty and Prophet etched in elegance
Meaning known to me and no other parkers
My symbol of belonging, for me not for them

My thoughts walk from my car to my office
With the day and the names two steps ahead
And I sit at my desk and gaze at that book's
Words climbing from two flower-framed pages
Politely letting a black ribbon rest for the day
While they nudge each other from right to left
And I lift my eyes from Your gift to us all
Through glass still wearing winter's stains to
Where pink popcorn droops above the car as
A sweet taste of the creation made in six days

Planned wisdom fills my mind in the morning
Yet drips wasted from my mouth as a leak and
I sigh my prayers to replace it whenever I notice
My humanity and the whisperer darkening
Dreams of Jannah in all-year blossom
And I walk at the end with smaller thoughts
To the car bursting with names (and a tassel)
And drive to where they ask what I did
The reply, oh you know, same as always,
Is truer than they could possibly know

Empty One

Whisperer oh whisperer
You have power in another world
That of crosses and doors into souls you can enter

Whisperer oh whisperer
You frighten them or take the blame
For what their own lust entices them to do

Flame without smoke
You cannot burn me for a second
Or brand my skin with a hiss to pretend I belong

Flame without smoke
You murmur and gossip too much
But I know your silent voice speaks like mine

Clay-hating shadow
I hear you as me almost all day
Yet I don't bother listening as often as I did

Clay-hating shadow
You choose your words carefully
Whispering sweet things you hope will work

Jinn named as shame
You have succeeded only rarely
When I let judgement slip as sand through fingers

Jinn named as shame
You hold no sway and cannot smile here
On this path your words stick as dust in your throat

Enticer going
Cringing as the day approaches
When the One will beckon while you wither and fade

Enticer gone
Heat extinguished by under-flowing waters
Thrown worthless into an undying death that chars

All in Their Eyes

You lower your eyes
Lashes shading secrets
Your hair unseen
And lips – are they smiling
Or pursed in sadness
Beneath a veil wrapped tight?

Your eyes open upwards
Darkened mines
Leading to a sacred place
For those needing peace
Where you sing to
Ease aches in old men

Your tears of blood
Don't fall when you blink
Or close tight for darkness
And strangers pass
Without stopping
To ask if you are lost

Black tears then flow
And you groan
As they form trails
On pale cheeks
Untouched
By the sun for years

Now they come to woo
Having seen you cry

And want to take you
As a lover although
You have covered and
Never shown your arms

I kiss my fingertips
Without sound
And yearn
To dab your face
Which I've known
As a guess in my mind

Oh Ummah my lady
They will bruise you
And lay you bare
While an unkind sun stings
Your beauty and steals
Such rare purity
Lower your gaze
Be true and hold fast
To your brothers and sons
As a cold wind calls them
To leave your home
And live among others

Oh Ummah beloved
Smile at your strength
Modesty shrouded
And don't let them know
The mysteries buried
In a heart cherished by God

From a Hadith

Two sat
Beneath the sun
In shade running off
An ageless wall
While all else
Vanished

One searched
The face of history
Saw worlds and between
In eyes that blinked
Occasionally

He saw himself
Mirrored alone
His cheeks burned
He shrank and looked
Away

The other
Raised an eyebrow
As a question
An invitation
Warm

The first stuttered
Overwhelmed
Asking for meaning
For the way to be
Wise

His life appeared
And galloped, flawed
Failing and struggling
Swallowing he looked
Down

Words came
From the other
Above a whisper
But not much and
Answered

Do not,
Said the wise,
Become angry
The path to wisdom
Lies in peace

The first asked again
His meaning lost?
The four words repeated
Were not to him
Enough

Do not,
Said the serene,
Become angry
The straight path
Is paved in patience

The first asked
With different words
The same a third time
Confused mind and ears
Unable

Do not,
Said the unwearied,
Become angry
The way to Jannah
Is for the gentle

Let it be for you

Ahl al-Kitab

Living waters sprang in widening rings
From Allah's word "Be!" and flowed
Through the words of a wanderer
Who broke idols which refused to speak
And Nile-wide and diamond pure it flowed
While Allah smiled and named the son
Father and *Khalil Allah* – the source
Of a swirling breathing river of blood
That carved canyons in time before
It forked

Down rapids one parted river ran
Carrying nations and prophets
Drowning rogues and doubters
Holding afloat a bobbing truth
Shema Yisrael God our Lord is One
Which reached and wet the ankles of
The anointed who agreed with thanks
And for three years past thirty proclaimed
After cupping his hands and drinking
Shema Yisrael God our Lord is One

Peace-sleeping stopped him seeing
The dirtying of that flow of silver life
As a brook from another source
Touched and joined and weakened
The truth which survived but struggled
Slipping under and seldom rising
As time pulled colour from the final word
And left the meaning faint and faded
Seen only by those who truly searched

From the fork the other branch flowed
Unnoticed by a world no longer caring
Until it reached the city of the blind
And lapped around that black cube

With a sound heard by one praying
Alone in a cave who descended
Drank and scooped to safety
The fragile truth which loving lips
Recited on command as a pleasure

The two are running closely apart to
The day when they will slip beneath
Jannah's jade carpet and cool shade
And one will arise as bubbling springs
Where the final word *Ehad, One, Ahad*
Lights the sky as seven swollen suns
And he smiles at those who stayed clean
With hands and hearts washed daily
By purity flowing around bent knees

Day of Judgement

I sat with the Mosque Chairman
Who teaches driving
And he searched me

I watched his unsure voice
Advancing certainly
Hoping to convince me

I looked from his coffee feet
Up to my pallid hands
Which pigeonholed me

I caught a mistake far too big
About the Ahl al-Kitab
Which bothered me

I heard no cold presumption
About a final hot abode

So this relieved me

I corrected with audacity
As he smiled patiently
And endured me

I quoted from Book and Prophet
Aware from an eyebrow
Of surprise at me

I shook his hand with fastened eyes
And finger-touched my heart
Really hoping he will use me

A Wind Blew

You spoke to me
As a murmur
Somewhere

You struck me
With my name
As a feather

I heard echoes
Lost my way
In circles

New whispers
Stopped me
Walking

Once more
I implored
Through years

A storm arose
Swept a name
Aloft

I reached up
Wanting it
Back

You lifted me
Up to You
Light

I held the name
So different
Yours

I speak with You
As a murmur
Everywhere

Libya

Firing from corners
Without aim

No soldier, you

Excited
Vengeful
Or

Wanting drama
Without death

No martyr, you

Careful
Frightened
Or

Aiming to live long
For children

No fool, you

Responsible
Altruistic
Or

Seeking the overdue
Risking darkness

No coward, you

Motivated
Inspired
Free

Battle of Misrata

No sleeping weeping dreaming
Homes cells living hells
Distress and yearning cars burning
Manic panic hatred volcanic
Guns clap slap clatter shatter
Shot hot screaming red streaming

Wards crowded bodies shrouded
Lost brothers mothers others
Shaken forsaken torn worn taken
Confusions doubts shouts transfusions
Sutures hurried, futures buried
Dying dead fear dread world worried

Civil war gore more vile not worthwhile
For ruins rubble endless trouble
City smashed trashed hopes dashed
But for ideas new frontiers end of tears
Tenacity audacity courage groping hoping
Must seek meet defeat fate hate and fears

Life as Childhood

As I beckoned to the horizon and plucked the rising sun
Swallowed it and guzzled the Atlantic to cool my burning throat
You spoke to my pride from inside a breadcrumb and said be
smaller

Like Alice I shrank as I spun and became nothing ... almost
I felt my heart swell and lift me as a balloon
To float through a vista of Your wonderland

Man Named Razi

Lost
Anywhere
In Pakistan
Called me Sir
On Facebook
Crushed
At 21
No Future
Typed tears
... At 21!

Seven billion
We two
Together

In single lines
Friends
With a click
Brothers
Forever
Insha'Allah

God is there
On Facebook
Everywhere
Reading
His words
And mine
The third
In our chat

His future?
You oh Lord
And mine!
He asked me
Remember
Duas please
Sir

Creator beloved
I see a photo
Small
In the corner
You see him
Knowing

Hope-bringer
I beseech you
For the boy
Who cries
On my screen

Lord of the Worlds
In Pakistan
Please
Touch

Hope for 22
Friend
And more

The future
Has five letters

Allah

Soon

No shadows fall in Jannah
No whispers ride the breeze
Sleep without nightmares
Doors unlocked
Walls without clocks
Ageless eyes smiling
Milk and sweet gold
No cigarette ash
Drunk on joy
One new race
Chosen people
Agreeing
An Ummah
Again
At last
And Him

You Kept Me

I pointed them
Slightly arched
Fingerprints
Fusing
A steeple

I cup them
Almost touching
As a boy
Waiting
To catch

I lowered my eyes
Crooked my neck
Or whispered
Before sleep
A little

I surrender
On the floor
Mind
Speaking
More

You preserved me
In a pocket
Secure
I lived
And am here

My time
For you
I am ready
Embarrassed
No more

Life in Gulps

I gagged
At the bitterness

Of the apple she gave
In a film to a girl who
Sung with sparrows
And cleaned

Sin stung
But I did not swallow

That polished orb
Red in the hand of
Death as a crone
Who lied

My head spun
For decades

As I wiped my lips and
Tongue on my sleeve
To rub off the taste
Of judgement impending

I spat without manners
Again again

This serpentine venom
That wanted to swim
In veins to my heart
With a wicked desire

I gulped the water
That I found

In a book that overflows
And spat again
Twice I think or thrice
Before swallowing

That shrivelled hand
No longer extends

Evil with a gleam
To my eyes but others
Choke daily after snatching
And ignoring sour warnings

Darling in Misrata

A Child
Caught a thing
Meant for another
It flew yet wasn't a bird
It whistled
She never heard

It tore her dress
Of blue cotton
And seven lives
Which must wait
Until Paradise
To be mended

Birds of the Battlefield

Bullets speak differently
when they meet someone new.

They scream "thwack!"
when they strike bone.

They shout "pthumpff!"
when they slap into thick muscle.

They squeal "pffit!"
when they pass through emptier flesh.

Best of all, they hiss "pzinnggg!" to themselves
when they find no-one to talk with.

What do they say

when they introduce

a new friend

to

death?

Nature

Seismic Tectonic
Quaking   Plates grinding   Shaking
Grating   Irritating   Great rift   Continental drift
Separating   Tearing   Shearing   Splitting   Fire-spitting
Unremitting Tough Rough Unproductive Self-destructive
Flashing   Crashing   Clashing   Dashing
Awful   Powerful   Wonderful
Infertile   Fruitful
Soothing Hurtful
Brightening
Frightening
Mystifying
Satisfying
Sustaining
Maintaining
Flawed Ummah Adored Ummah

His Face

Behind glass
wiped

religiously

a fragile
page
in blue
and gold

showed
a face of
flames

In another,

emptiness
white

beneath
a fiery
turban

In a third,

a veil and
black
hair
blazing

In a newspaper,

a bomb
with a
fuse

hissing

Today

You are a Muslim?
Wow!
flashed
a text

On my iPhone
from a
very
dear
friend

He knew
for a year
or more

I thought

Honestly

He didn't

Until he
read
a
BBC
Website

My thumb
tapped

a

☺

Honestly

More Life as Childhood

You rolled me as a glass marble from your thumb
Onto a yellow road along which I've skipped for years
Away from shadows and the ordinary in black and white
Toward something gleaming beyond all else

No-one speaks into a tube and winds a handle
The protective walls in emerald are truth in love as
Whispered words that beat from Your book like
Migrating butterflies – monarchs – during Spring

For What?

Seventeen in Marrakesh
Sipping beauty
And coffee

Children and mums
In pieces

The deaf

The blind

And torn

Closer to the God
Who loves
Innocence

A smell of hate
And heat
Survived

The
Angry blink

That Seventeen

Could not

Every Morning

Sin spirals quickly into the drain
Like an out-of-luck money spider
Pulling my shame to God knows where
Rinsed from my hair thrice
From a plastic jug made to measure
Ingredients in her kitchen

Hands and feet right to left
Again again drowning thieves unseen
That tried to clutch fair hairs on my arms
Everything swabbed like the deck
Of a flagship before a captain's inspection

Far greater comes on folded knees
After that baptism and a rub with a towel
And the donning of modesty chosen
Most days by another and laid on my bed

Oh Allah my Admiral match water and gold soap
With forgiveness and restoration in the depths
Let my sins spiral out from repentant groans inside
Pulling my shame to God knows where

Suicide Bomber

What did it take?

A beautiful boy packed tight
With no hint of a man's chin
By his dad who
Kissed him goodbye
With a hope of seeing him later

What did he know?

Carrying a sunburst in canvas
To strangers who never noticed
That their end stood five-feet-two
With a running nose
And a mind full of his mum

What was he thinking?

Avoiding all eyes as he stood
Among them with a small chest
That felt ready to explode
With the pressure of keeping
A secret for moments more

What would he think?

His life now a curling photo on a shelf
In a home where a family once laughed
And dust on a street where people still
Buy drinks, phone covers and fruit

Osama bin Laden

When I was a boy
I loved

The Phantom

In a cave

The Ghost who Walks

Today they killed
Another

Ghost who walks

Not one I loved

Living soft in town

And shown
Unmasked

On CNN

But can a ghost die?

Bin Laden: An End?

An age pierced his brain
and passed with him

A decade in a flicker

He dropped and we snatched him
hoping he would sink
somewhere

But maybe an age is harder
to kill

Today wears a coat
smeared with yesterday

Will the sunrise be red?

God's Blessings

"Are we ok?"
You ask though we are

always

And you cuddle

Squeezy

Like you did at seven
when you talked about hair
as you still do

You love to wind me up
Hate it when it works

"I haven't annoyed you, have I?"

"No, not yet."

> Our eyes
>   the same
>   smile

You have prattled
a river forever

Sometimes
I drift

Yet I know that one day
as I die
I'll need you there

– and I'll live for every word

The Journey Back

In the belly of the whale
I curled as

a not-yet within a mother

shivering with pain I couldn't feel
and called your name once

through the starless space
of titanic depth

You asked your slate gray friend
to rise as a filling balloon

from the crushing weight
of mistakes grown from knowledge
without experience

and sent me sprawling

I blinked blind in a sun forgotten
that burned some shame off my skin

as I coughed away my drowning
for six years then three

and looked inland for the meaning
of a second life apparently here

You had heard

You had accompanied me

always inside my shallow breaths

and waited for my groan to climb
a ladder from what felt dead

deep within a broken shell

I heard a call in a windless breeze that bore

my name as a seagull's caw
and my purpose as a kiss of clarity

And I call Yours again: Allah

Praying as a Revert

My eyes seek
solitude
in the depths of prayer

unconsciously

A habit
of decades
of darkness

Hard to break

I find You easier
with them closed
and wonder

when I shouldn't

why I shouldn't

and what brothers think
why their eyes watch mine

when they shouldn't

Yesterday

You owned that second
when I could do
nothing

You ruled the world
as the road shrank
in my eyes

You Oh Allah
were my seatbelt
which held

You were the airbag
that loved me
in a flash

You were all and above
when I slid
as nothing

You whispered hush
and steel noise and glass
complied

You Oh Allah
took no life there
nor let me

You control the heavens
earth and in-between
and You decide

Can I ever repay
You for a blink
of lasting life?

Holy Qur'an

When I let my eyes

fall
      into
            its
                 wisdom

I don't hear my voice
inside but

an angelic Lily Afshar
playing guitar with her eyes
closed

gently

and singing

note perfect

in the Irish flute voice
of that shaven-headed girl
who tore a photo of
some pope

The dancing of meaning
inside somewhere
changes me like ...

nothing I can describe

and I can't say
what I want except
to be prophetwise
and to gain Your smile

So I read and

sink
      within
            its
                 magic

Too Often

Shaytan winks

Within ...

a market
a boy
a vest
two wires
a second
a hole
a mistake
a crime

a sin

The Moment ... in Jakarta

Shopping for carved mahogany
In a crowd's foreign pandemonium
Searching

An eagle triumphant
For my desk

You stopped me

And pointed

To the wonder of
Undulating batik backs
Beneath wide stairs
In some convention centre

It transfixed me

Four hundred
Foreheads reached the carpet
And You

Oh I stared

Oh I knew

There I belonged

Lamentations

What possessed me
To sin like that?

Regret sighs
And I look down

I hide my eyes
As a child avoiding dad's

I can't turn them from You
You are everywhere

What possessed me
To welcome shame?

I breathe out
After a slow inhale

I try not to focus
And I want my mind to wander

A lead-heavy clarity within
Reminds me that You expect more

What possessed me
To act as though You weren't here?

You never leave or step further
Than an eyelash fallen on my cheek

I don't want my end to come
In this moment

How could I face You
And say I did it knowing You saw?

No Despair in Lamentations

You swooped and caught me
Knowing I would trip, stumble and fail

You heard my sorrowful lament
Before my lips formed words

You understood my thoughts
Before I even thought them

From the instant my soul began to groan
Your tender fingers touched my chest

Before defeat could overcome me
You told me I had the hope of triumph

I cupped my hands in prayer
And they were already full of grace

The moment I inhaled for astagfirullah
You placed peace within my lungs

The Cleft

In a desert midnight no darker than dawn
With cloudless heavens evident and stretching
To the edges of Bedouins' minds and ours
Where owls govern with Your permission

You plunged a mighty fist deep
Into the heart and gripped a molten rag
And pulled it into a peak of crags
In which the gash You wanted grew

With a rush of wind you shaped that
Tear into a world-sized hollow to shelter
A man and a starfilled future for any who
Might accept what tugged at him that night

You once said Be! and time commenced
But earlier you had chosen from first
Until final a stream of Rusul and You placed
In that cleft the last Rasul alone but never

And in the radiance of a challenging word
Your spirit whose wings dripped pearls
Asked the silent one who sailed in prayer
To revolve the world on a different axis

Running feet across the earth carried him
To the comfort of arms that felt a beating
Chest bursting with ten million truths and her
Assurances trounced the whisperer's last ditch

Words of mercy flow around us through a gentle
Heart in a stone cavity in the shade of a night
Without shadows beneath a cloudless cover
Which owls rule ... for a shrinking time

Will I Write a Poem about Her and Sin?

Shaytan murmured
Write a poem about her!
I started
Words flowed
And were good

A muse! Such allure!

"You came and stood close
And I so wished my eyes
Weren't red
From writing
My lecture
Late at night"

Allah said
Don't type any more

So I didn't

It wasn't good

I dragged the cursor
Across the rest
With restraint and
What-ifs
Then tapped

Delete

Regret in Cashmere

A stubbled beggar with a faded mutt
Pressing tight and a hungry brown hat
I think holding coins three of four
In winter's pain of frozen lungs
And a running nose wiped on
A sleeve said "Your coat looks warm"
While I walked wrapped smiling in
Cashmere black and warm except
My heart which pushed flippant words
"So does yours" from lips that
Still tasted of red sweets from
The cinema but the stabbing lance
Of conscience that pierced my side
Told me like a nana's sermon that I had
Ignored Allah's words and walked too
Far in a coat meant for the one who could
Not buy what I could: another

In Different Rooms

I choose solitude

They watch television
Downstairs

I bend as they recline

I place my mind on a mat
While theirs slip through adverts
About cat food and sofas

I whisper to You of truth and grace
While they discuss invented worlds
And cockney characters

Seclusion is never forlorn
We are together

As they are
Downstairs

And I love them

The World is an Asian Intersection

Holding out
An empty baby

Monkeylike
Two months old or nine
Dusty, limp and sun-dried

A desiccated mother
Large teeth missing
Appears at the window
With a bonelike hand cupped
Within the opportune moment
Offered by a red light and begs
For her God's provision

A fully-toothed driver
Eased by his creator
And the tired air-con
Warns the torn and shocked
Who shrinks in comfort
In the cream leather back
About the fine he'd pay if he
Slipped her a note of
No known value
To lengthen life
And please the lover
Of mothers

Ambrosia

I sipped Ayat al-Kursi

          swirled it inside

Seven sweet seconds

Savouring before

          a swallow
          felt ever so
          warm

It reached my head

Was I drunk?

Such Power

She acted her iman in forty-one
Covered Facebook photos for 2,431
Friends and she looked like a Muslimah
Should and built a wall of pious bricks

But after burning all Israelis
With kerosene-soaked words

And when she graffitied
"I f---ing hate that b--ch Lady Gaga!!!"
On her wall

And seven bearded friends liked it and
Weighed in with their own
Hard-knuckled violence

Another pulled his lips tight and made her
Extinct with a single press and
Now he can't even remember
His friend's angry name

Everything

You have ninety-nine names of splendour
I am Abdullah

You are greater than all universes and anything beyond
I stand five foot seven

You are infinite and time fits within Your palm
While my hair grows grey

You are magnificent and ever so flawless
My feet get too hot in summer

And I sometimes snore (so I'm told)

You see everything always
My eyes get red from too much reading

But I study Your book – religiously

You understand far more than all knowledge
I don't even know where Moldova is

Without searching Wikipedia

You parted the sea and split the moon
While I get tired carrying groceries

You answer millions of prayers – billions? – at once
Yet I can't follow television when my daughter chatters

But I listen to Shoshana (usually)

You created her and Michaela
I am merely their adoring father

I am Abdullah
You are everything
I am happy

At the Office on Thursday

The Ambassador and I
spoke Arabic and I
led him in

Nearly all I knew lasted the
feeling of a rushed breath
but was more

It was a lot to one who had
not talked easily
all day

His grin stretched when
he heard Ana Muslim
Alhamdulillah

The Undersecretary of
State's astonishment
blinked

Two shared as brothers
while a Lord in
pinstripes smiled

The Ambassador's state
of rocks and sand loved
by three grew

Two Muslims and
a wide-eyed mandarin
pulled lands together

My office glowed with a
Surah's truth
and I thanked You

Everywhere

Susurrating grass, the sway of pliant poplars and nodding
Leaves on a creeper which presses against the window
Whisper something sweet that exists in every single thing

A cracked mountain's exhaust pumps like a dying
Chevrolet something eternal into an unloving
Cloud of ash through which birds won't fly

A silver school twisting like a ribbon or a bed-sheet
Deep yet where light rays illuminate its movement
Lives to tell oceans about something exalted

Sparrows fluttering nervously up and back from the
Old bread left near the clothes line by a grandmother
Blink a message in beady eyes like Morse code

Something perfect comes as a reply from the wings
Of locusts that steal almost all life from fields of hope
Sown by those whose children emerge without sin

And the slow drip of bluish water from a frozen point
Within a glacial cave creates a cadence that beats
Something healing at the pace of a turtle's heart

The too-often cough of a smoking uncle holds the purity
Of something living that swirls then vanishes
As it holds aloft the vitalising glory of its owner

Even evil flying from an assassin's rifle can't sully the
Perfection of the Name carried with the prior knowledge
Of the One who will roll up time with justice read from a book

Born with a Burden

The
Left-handed
Revert
Weighs more
Before
And during

A meal
With friends
Than
After

And

Can't
Forget that
Receiving
Requires
As much
Thought
As giving

Muslim Youth Workshop

Innocent eyes and bright. One hundred pearls
For a speaker who loves the future. He posed
A question.

How many of you have read
Harry Potter? ... The first one.

Hesitation climbed
From curiosity. A trick question?
Advancing teenage years bought the fear of
Embarrassment.

Ok, how many of you once read
It ... when you were younger?

Everyone raised
A hand; well, almost.

From cover to cover?

Yes, they kept them high.
77,000 words were apparently
No great challenge. Alhamdulillah.

They looked
At each other, pleased.

Great; next question:
How many of you have read the Holy Qur'an?

Even in English is fine.

Gosh. Very few hands now.

From cover to cover?

None; well, almost.

A different set of words – 77,000 also –
Had less magic for these young Muslims
Than a boy with a lightening scar.

Teenage discomfort reached the roof. They
Understood the speaker's challenge. Alhamdulillah.

Unfathomable Depths

To take the life of any Innocent
– so treasured by You –
Is to rob the breath of all who live
But Your mercy is such

Ya Rahman
Ya Rahim

That if he had asked You

Truly

You would even have absolved
And welcomed
To You
That one who
Choked six million worlds

If he had asked

Truly

Life is Such

I slept smiling
And you were with me
In my thoughts
When I should have
Had none

You brought morning
Through gaps between
My curtains and
Appeared – wondrous –
In my first flickers
Of light

You watched me all day
And when I felt your
Gaze I wandered
For a few long
Seconds

And wondered how
You saw anything
When I have
Seen nothing
Worth much
At all

You touched me
Deeply with
Gentle words
That I repeated
During my solitary
Moments

When your patience
With my failings
And your doting
Reassurances
Eased the pain
Of regrets

My day
Has been yours
And as I wait
For darkness I
See you somewhere
And think of
Tomorrow

The Fifth That Day

He was the fifth
On the seventh
Of the seventh

I never liked him
But those four saw
Something I did not

They hadn't known
Him for that long
Not from boyhood

He sure had it
The gift of the gab
My dad would say

He told stories
That gave them
Such dreams

Let's do something!
Be someone! We
Can! We really should!

They planned a trip
To the city and
Asked him to come

He liked July
He liked the city
He liked them too

He grinned and chatted
As they descended the
Escalators

They hung by hand
Straps squeezed in
The heat with strangers

He had helped them
To pack and then to
Carry their bags

He said goodbye
To three and went
Off to find the other

He joined that one
The youngest
Elsewhere upstairs

He told him too
I'll see you later
And he meant it

Such good friends
They had
Become

All those hours
In the kitchen
Making mess

Those quiet moments
Of mateship
Now gone

Making friends
Is never easy
For most

Yet he seemed
To have no
Problems

That fifth on
The seventh
Of the seventh

With the four
Gone he's back
To his old tricks

He's made
New mates
Already

Have you heard
Who? I
Haven't

But Allah has
Somewhere
Ready for them

Ideal for that
Whispering liar
Made from a flame

And any new friends
Who might take him
Dead seriously

The No. 30 in Tavistock Square

"You're better off walking!" he called
From behind the wheel on any day
And fifty oh so lucky left the red tin –
Seconds before it ripped open – so
They could escape jams in an old city
Bleeding within its bowels after three
White seconds split apart a single
Minute that had already lasted forever

George hadn't seen young
Hasib's eyes and newish beard
And other passengers ignored the
Boy-man with the pack and didn't
Notice if he was torn until they
Saw him torn and vanishing from
The world of cricket and football
And driving lessons from his dad

Hasib wasn't seeing the world that
Day and he felt very small and
The world became so much smaller
As he sat close among women and
Strangers who could not see
The black emptiness in the heart
He called a warrior's in a lie
To himself and to God

He stopped lying when he and
Thirteen others left amidst a shower
Of red metal and red liquid that
Fell across the universe from
The top deck of an icon full of
Innocence and innocents
In a burst of burning air that
Shrank as a pricked balloon

I can't get on a train! he had breathed
By phone to the three dead who
Had already departed London with
Thirty-nine others who had not
Wanted to leave and he took his
Bulk into the belly of George's realm
So that he could earn his stripes

Calls to his friends who were
Missing for fifty minutes went
Nowhere because they were nowhere
And he knew that his moment
Of emulation had arrived in
A bus in a square in a sin that
Only he inhabited among those
Who wanted to work or shop

George will never be the
same and Hasib will never be
Anything and the thirteen
Will live forever in memories
While the hate inside a large
Leeds lad that pulled apart
Muslims and others evaporated
With him and cannot touch us

Muslim Warrior

With cut-and paste ahadith that you've clearly hurled
As grenades in previous battles (it seems you won one
And enjoyed its sweetness) you waged war from the bunker of
Soft and safe self-righteousness plonked in front of a screen
In some estate in Scotland to prove that Jihad is Qital
And must be waged against those who exploit us – your enemies
Include our state that has let you swell and puff and
Enjoy such combat – and your soldierly aggression was such
That I couldn't help wondering why you have never taken
That anger and valour over to where you can risk your skin
Rather than trying to earn martyrdom with inflamed courage
By defeating me on Facebook

Mortal Dread

An email flew from a
Graceless yesterday
Lodging deep
And he groaned
Falling forward
Staring at a portent

He pulled the arrow's shaft
And a trickle of pain
Ran down his exposed breast
But he pressed
His palm and prayed

Oh Allah what have I done?
Have I not paid
Enough?

You have paid a full price
And justice asks
For nothing now

He read and tears fell
Upon his keyboard
And he thanked
The one who shot for
Aiming so well

A dove flew from his fingers
Returning with
Noah's sign and
He sighed
Giving thanks
And embraced truth

We Talk

It kills me that you
Say I was born into sin
When my sister
Died at birth

It kills me that you
Say the unborn
And everliving
Died for three days

It tears me in two
When you count
Some One as
Three

I'm gutted that
You say I
Have lost
My soul

Yet I take heart
That the Almighty
Sees what beats
Within me

And I can't begin to
Tell you of my
Wonder that He is
Beyond description

Love as I Write

How is it that I
Cannot bear the thought
Of living without my
Heart's great love
Although I have never seen
Your smile or held your hand
Heard the softness of your words
Smelled your subtle fragrance
Or felt your fingers reassure
My hair like mum once did?

How is that you love me
And tenderly reach to hug
Me when I need it though I
Bring shame so often and
You hear my worst and see
Even those things I would
Hide if I could but I can't and
You know that sometimes

My thoughts wander
Where they shouldn't?

What should I tell them
When they ask why
I'm smiling to myself
And should I let them in
On the secret that I'm
Never alone and that within
The greying of shrinking time
My heart beats like a fifth-
Former with a note passed
From a dreamed sweetheart?

Why would I keep
You to myself when I know
That you wrote that note
In surahs for all who need
What they don't know is
Beyond a father's wisdom
A motherly embrace
A warm drink in dark winter
A cool swim in summer
And an offer of foreverness?

Noodles in Jakarta

You walked out on your husband because
Allah wanted you to be happier

You chased some illusion of romance
That He truly had in mind for you

You left the son you adopted so
That Allah would make you a real mum

You didn't have to search that hard
Because He would bring you a job

And if He didn't it was because He
Had a new husband with money waiting

But

Paradise – said our Prophet
– is at the feet of mothers

And you now live alone in a single room
That smells of instant noodles

For Her in That Room

Oh Allah

Let those stumbled
Steps of foolishness
Lead to a path
Paved in better
Judgement

I did not pray for those
Things she wanted

How could I?

But I do now

Send her someone

If that's Your will

Please

Oh Allah, if her eyes will enlarge
In her world that has shrunk
And her lips will caress Your names

Won't you wrap her in soft compassion?

Through Time

A joy still spreads in frog-coloured greenness from a parched
Slab of a camel desert

Springs in souls rise as Zamzam's laughter beneath the ardent
Stare of an encroaching sun in a cloudless unflawed stripe

The clearest voice once sang as a happy tenor inside a
Cave too small for echoes

Words of resonant depth joined and forever swell a chorus of
Worship sung by those who remain close when darkness comes

Prayers grin at gravity as they skip up spiralling staircases to their
Owner who has never misplaced or overlooked a single sigh

He smiles at all green-croaking devotions and invites the
Ones who glimmer in His eyes to journey up if they will

Qabil and Habil

Sons of the same great pawing lion
Who yawned contentedly and watched
You joy in bringing the hint of meaning
To a mother's Mona Lisa smile

You wrestled and grew strong like
Mongols on the hard steppes
And you laughed when you fell
Upon each other in young-muscled
Slips of twisting balance

When the whisperer crouched close
And said who was strongest it was a lie
Borrowed from lofty circling vultures
And you should not have looked
At each other in that way

Will jealousy fill your mind, brother
Hamas, with pulsing thoughts of his
Quiet nature so admired? Calm your soul
And look! He has eyes just like yours

Will feelings of weakness make your
Chest tight and your knuckles white,
Dear Fatah? Strengthen your spirit, look
In the mirror and quietly call, "Akhi"

Return to your wrestling and press
Your wet hair together in tight squeezes
Of brotherhood and grow stronger
In love

And present that as a single offering
With the Ummah's prayers that it will
Reach and please the One who
Called that tawny lion Ibrahim His friend

Oh champion of the sad and hurt we beseech
You to accept their fragrantly full salver
And to strengthen their memories of youth
Whenever the slitherer slips out greenish words

History can be written on different scrolls and
That crying blow need not fall if they will make pride
A sworn foe and return to their flocks and fields
With something for their mother's lips

Jihad al-Nafs

I confront my antagonist and
Demand with a poke what Allah wants:

My release from his clutch

He has pursued me
Plagued and poisoned me

Lifted me then cast me
Down

I have turned from him
Fled and he has followed

His hot breath on my neck drove me
Like a wrathful wind in a whipping sail

I need him gone and
My soul unbound

For calm to flatten the sea

To hold my enslaver's familiar stare
And shake myself free

I must die to me so that I can live
And you can smile

I burn my desires upon a pyre
And pour Allah's will over the dying cinders

Prophethood

You are a shepherd

A lamb

> *Sweethearted*

A fisherman

Loaves and fishes

The salt of the earth

You are an ark

A dove returning

An olive branch

A rainbow

Stained glass windows

The chiming of bells

The good news

> *You are*

> *Muhammadur Rasulullah*
> *Sallallahu alayhi wa sallam*

Capturing Beauty

Wizened and white
He ached
As he always did
To paint the glory
Of radiant Allah
Subhanahu wa Taʿala
With a palette
Of dazzling colours

His thin fingers
Held a thinner brush
And faded yellowing eyes
Delighted in the brightness
Of the harvest colours
Already toothpaste-
Squeezed onto his
Waiting mixing board

And he wondered
What should emerge
This time
From his canvas as
An offering to the one
Who gave him a steady
Hand now trembling
And a keen eye

After having captured
Creation as a master
For forty years
He thought again
As he always did
Of what beauty
Might exceed what
He'd ever seen

But he found nothing
Again in his mind's
Eye more precious
Than the memory
Of a melting red sunset
When he once strolled
With sandy feet
In love and with
A firm hand wrapped
Around his long-dead
Wife's

And he smiled and
Gave thanks to the one
Who had created
Far greater suns than
That one and scattered
Them as pebbles
Through the widening
Universe with a simple
Clear thought

And he returned his brush
Undipped to the jar
That had always
Welcomed it home and
Ran fingertips lovingly
Over an empty canvas
That danced with joy
When he spoke with
A quiver, "Oh Allah"

"What could I paint
With my hands
That could equal
Those words?"

And he sat
On a cane chair
With creaks
Bowed his neck and
Painted perfection
With thanks for his
Life and his wife's
With a rainbow of
Words – *"La ilaha
Illallah Muhammadur
Rasulullah"* –
That flowed from
Scarcely open
Lips while he
Looked at his bare canvas
And saw God's beauty
In its emptiness

Insha'Allah

Oh Ibrahim, God's friend,
What would you now say
To those who have chosen
That star unknown to the
King with the sling whose
Name deserves better?

He slew jeering Jalut
And ruled with wisdom
And never sought to have
Enemies caged and
Humiliated if they
Could live as neighbours

Oh cherished Ibrahim,
What would you say
To those who have done
That to a nation with
The name not nature
Of bronzed Jalut's kin?

Confined lions pacing
Always hungry in a
Cage too small snarl
When poked with sticks by
Those who seem wildly
Confused by their triumph

And the keepers cry
Oh look at their ravenous
Eyes and tearing teeth
And see why they
Can never be released
Back into nature

Oh Ibrahim, what
Would you do if you
Learned that Ishaq's
Left hand had
Bound Isma'il
In knots too tight?

Would you tell us
Whether the right hand
Knows what the left
Hand does and whether
The right will ever
Actually do what is right?

Great God we offer pleas
For the deliverance
Of the forlorn encaged
Who pace in circles and see
The opportunity of freedom
In an open world beyond bars

It's Monday Tomorrow

A pigeon came as grace from God at six
And walked rainwet on my windowsill. Did he
Also bring a mild rebuke? One orangey eye
Then the other warned me that last week
Must not become this week.

Jinns of smokeless fire had pulled down
Around us such a thunderfilled cloud
That summer shivered within its darkness
And we became colder. We bickered. Want
That shadow gone enough and it will be,
The ringnecked and orange promised.

They had whispered to the worst aspects within
Us which proved vulnerable to the stings of
Pridewounding rumours. Recognise their voices,
He said, which are not your own, and ignore them.
They did their jobs by convincing you both that you
Are not very good at doing yours.

Yunus Found in Darkness

Foul smell he wore, dead sea and more
He gagged upon wet sand
With lungs aching and tongue burning
Tight and cramping stomach churning
He felt the land, the land.

Salt-fighting eyes blinked in white pain
The sun jabbed aches into his brain
A man who thought he'd gone insane
He looked back at the sea
With death now fought, Oh Lord, he thought
Your monster has saved me.

Its ancient bulk slid further out
Through waves called in by birds
Which gave gratitude in screeches
For braving such shallow beaches
To obey Allah's words.

Leviathan, with his task done
Slipped deep into the black
With a cavernous draw of air
An hour of life, unspoken prayer
Then up and back, and back.

I have not yet shared all I know
Of those events so long ago
Which brought salvation after woe
Hearken to this story
Us it reaches, us it teaches
God earns all the glory.

How did he know he was chosen
To call the wrong to right?
What type of guidance made him shake?
Did its gravity make him quake?
What made him start his flight?

The task too great, he fled his fate
Which found him in that hour
When Allah used his strength as Lord
To frighten all who sailed aboard
Who cried, Such power! Such power!

With howling winds and cries of fear
They raised curses into the air
Their minds overcome with despair
As the storm closed it grip
Drowning the wails, ripping the sails,
And tearing at the ship.

Did he know that Allah wanted
Only a change of thought?
Did he see the Creator's hand?
Would his confused mind understand?
Would he do what he ought?

The crew loud yelled, he still rebelled
In madness and torment
While stinging salt spray screamed in ears
And dreadful minutes passed as years
Winds cried: repent, repent!

The storm's anger set minds aflame
Hot with thoughts of who was to blame
Who on board had a secret shame?
The cursed must give his life
So they threw dice, their hearts of ice
And chose their sacrifice.

They threw him into the wild sea
Cold gasping he sank down
For their gods to leave them alone
They had chosen one to atone
And he would have to drown.

In pitch black ink, where he did sink
He had no chance of help
But Allah sent his monstrous beast
Which opened for a man-sized feast
And gave a gulp, a gulp.

Its stinking gut became a womb
The living cave became a room
For one who thought it was a tomb
He gagged in caustic air
Choked out a plea, Lord please save me!
And begged God to be there.

Forgive my failings mighty Lord
Please let me live not die
I will obey your every word
I will do everything I heard
Grant me the chance to try.

With throat burning and soul yearning
He felt tears freely run
A weight of pain and shame combined
It almost overwhelmed his mind
He gasped, You're One, the One.

Great Allah told his giant friend
That the Prophet's torments should end
And to his task he should attend
So to shore the whale turned
Thrilled to do right, filled with delight
That he had God's joy earned.

The one inside also rejoiced
That he had gained God's grace
He felt it change his very core
Which clean it washed forever more
From feelings of disgrace.

They surged to shore, eager and more
To serve the One who saves
Focused in a sea of purpose
Two as one beneath the surface
Under the waves, the waves.

I have already shared with you
About that blessed retch or two
Which on the beach a prophet threw
The world's most famous cough
Gentle and calm, to do no harm
Was thank God not too rough.

Our story has not yet ended
The rest should now be learned
About how one man changed many
Taught a city of blind to see
And God's loving smile earned.

Within a week, no longer meek
He had regained his voice
To those who had rejected truth
He shouted with the zeal of youth
You have no choice, no choice!

Obey the Lord and bow your knees
Offer your sorry prayers in pleas
Cry to Him your apologies
Don't let a moment pass
Without reprieve, you must believe
That judgement's coming fast.

My God, the one thrown in the sea
Has come back from the dead
We had rejoiced at his demise
Yet here he is with fire in eyes
They cried aloud in dread

In shock and fear, it became clear
That they could not ignore
A prophet drowned far out at sea
Was back – alive – in their city
Demanding more, much more!

City elders were first to bow
Swayed by unimagined power
They repented that very hour
With their glad young and wives
They sank right there and offered prayer
And thanked God for their lives.

In time they all heeded the call
And Allah they obeyed
Their prophet taught them all wisdom
Through many years of joy with him
And endlessly they prayed.

Let us give praise, God's name let's raise
For sending loved Yunus
With clear guidance on how to live
And with God's perfect grace to give
With love to us, for us.

From So Far Away

Who is it that speaks from time to time
Hesitantly and with such long pauses
On the phone some Sundays?

I recognise the cough

Sixty years of twenty a day have
Placed a grim sign of the future
Within a throat beneath a jaw
That sags in last year's photo
The voice reminds me of a memory

Forty years of quick words
Without hesitation flowing from
A bright untaught mind that should
Have thought and given more

Who has stolen my father
And replaced him with a strangely
Slow old man who seems to know me?

The stillness on the phone disturbs me

A childhood of outbursts and shaking
Emotion sometimes aimed my way
Is fading fast in a mind confused by
Time and this imposter's blandness

His words aren't familiar

The real McCoy wouldn't risk the
Words "I love you" – at least not on me –
As he once did on a boy ready for sleep
Beneath an orange candlewick bedspread

Such shrinkage really frightens me

A room full of evident vigour that
Sometimes whipped us as a tempest
Now feels like a shoe-box
Of trapped air

Who will give me the courage to ask
That deflated and tired voice if he
Knows that I have always forgiven him?

Oh Allah I ask for a braver heart
To push from my lips my three best words
To that truly beloved ancient stranger
Who still calls me sometimes on a Sunday

Sajjadah in My Quietest Place

Why do I think of another?

You are still lovely to touch
And have shared my truest
Fears and joys for years

You have grown old yet so have I
And my dreamy stare remembers
More than traces of your beauty
Which is delicate and faded

You have listened without
Condemning me when
My heart has broken
And I have confided failings

With exhaled deep breaths
Of shame I have admitted things
That should perish in flames
And my tears have touched you

You don't look like you did
And my burden has aged you
Yet you have borne my love and
The softest sounds I can make
And where my knees have rested
Your woven pile is worn and you shine
Flattened where my head and hands
Have met you in my deepest moments

Glossary of Arabic Words and Phrases

Abdullah
Servant of God

Ahad
One, as in God's indivisible unity

Ahadith
Plural of hadith

Ahl al-Kitab
The People of the Book: the Jews and Christians to whom scriptures were revealed by God through the Prophets

Akhi
My brother

Al-Furqan
The Criterion (the Holy Qur'an itself)

Alhamdulillah
Praise be to God!

Allahu Akbar
God is greatest!

Ana Muslim
I am a Muslim

Astagfirullah
I seek God's forgiveness, or God forgive me

Ayat al-Kursi
The Verse of the Throne – *Surah al-Baqarah* 2:255 – which is considered to be the greatest verse in the Holy Qur'an

Deen
Religion, meaning Islam

Duas
Prayers, supplications

Ehad
The Hebrew word for "one," as in God's indivisible unity

Fatah
A Palestinian political party

Hadith
A saying or teaching of the Prophet Muhammad

Halal
Something allowed in Islam

Hamas
A Palestinian political party

Ibrahim
Abraham

Iman
Faith

Insha'Allah
If God wills

Isa
Jesus

Ishaq
Isaac

Isma'il
Ishmael

Jalut
Goliath

Jannah
Heaven or Paradise

Jihad
Struggle or exertion. This can be a struggle against armed attack, serious direct persecution or religious oppression. It mainly refers to an individual's struggle to overcome the imperfections of his or her human nature (i.e., Jihad al-Nafs).

Jihad al-Nafs
The struggle against one's carnal nature

Jinn
Elemental spirits created from fire

Khalil Allah
Friend of God: a phrase used to describe Abraham

Marrakesh
A city in Morocco.

Misrata
A city in Libya.

Muhammadur Rasulullah
Muhammad the Prophet of God

Musa
Moses

Muslimah
Female Muslim

Misbahah beads
A misbahah is a string of traditional prayer beads which some Muslims use to remember Allah, send salutations to the Prophet, seek forgiveness and so on.

Qabil and Habil
Cain and Abel

Qital
Combat, fighting. It can be a form of righteous struggle as part of a war waged defensively and according to just principles.

Quraysh
The dominant tribe in Mecca during the lifetime of the Prophet Muhammad

Rabbana Lak al-Hamd
A praising sentence within the daily prayers ("Our Lord, Praise be to You!")

Rasul
A Prophet and Messenger of God.

Rusul
Plural of Rasul

Sajjadah
Prayer mat

Sallallahu alayhi wasallam
Peace and blessings upon him (said after the name of Muhammad)

Shahadah
The Islamic testimony of faith that there is no God except God and that Muhammad is the Prophet of God

Shaytan
Satan, the devil

Shema Yisrael
"Shema Yisrael" (Hebrew for "Hear, Oh Israel") are the first two words of an illustrious biblical verse (Deuteronomy 6:4) that encapsulates Judaism's and Christianity's monotheistic essence: "Hear, Oh Israel, the Lord our God the Lord is One."

Subhanahu wa Ta'ala
May He be glorified and exalted

Subhana Rabbi al-A'la
A praising sentence within the daily prayers ("Glory to my Lord the Most High")

Surah
The Holy Qur'an has 114 Surahs (chapters).

Thawr
The Prophet Muhammad and his close companion Abu Bakr famously hid from enemy soldiers in a cave within Mount Thawr during their migration to Medina in September 622.

Uhud
The Battle of Uhud, fought in March 625, was the second large battle fought between the Prophet Muhammad and his warriors and an army sent by Mecca to destroy the Muslims. The Prophet was wounded during the battle.

Ummah
The Community (of Muslim believers everywhere)

Ya Rahim
Oh Ever-Merciful (God)

Ya Rahman
Oh Most Compassionate (God)

Yunus
Jonah

Yusuf
Joseph

Zamzam
The Well of Zamzam is a spring located near the Kaaba (the ancient black cube-shaped building in Mecca), which is the holiest place in Islam. According to Islamic belief, God brought forth a gush of water from the earth when Abraham's thirsty infant son Ishmael kept crying for water and kicking the ground.

Zuhr Prayer
One of the five obligatory daily prayers

SHADES OF ISLAM
POEMS FOR A NEW CENTURY

Rafey Habib

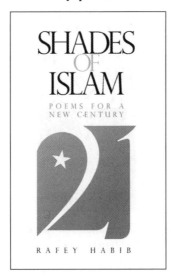

Shades of Islam is a dazzling collection of poetry that addresses faith, love, politics and Islam in the twenty-first century.

Rafey Habib is Professor of English at Rutgers University, and this is his first poetry collection.

"The poems of Rafey Habib offer a window into the sensibility of a modern American Muslim, with unflinching honesty and richly informed compassion. The great humanistic tradition of poetry known in Arabic and other Eastern languages here finds a contemporary English voice, which will be recognized like a lost friend who has unaccountably been rediscovered."

Carl W. Ernst
William R. Kenan, Junior, Distinguished Professor of Religious Studies, UNC-Chapel Hill

Xvii + 108pp, paperback
UK £8.99 | US $16.00
ISBN 978-1-84774-021-2

FOR WHOM THE TROUBADOUR SINGS
COLLECTED POETRY AND SONGS

Dawud Wharnsby

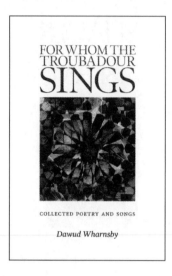

For Whom the Troubadour Sings collects together all the lyrics that have inspired faith communities around the world for over two decades.

Dawud Wharnsby has pioneered the English-language spiritual hymn (*nashid*) that draws upon Qur'anic teachings, with over 15 recordings since 1995.

"Dawud Wharnsby's poems are the very essence of a spiritual journey — words for our minds and words for our hearts."

Tariq Ramadan
Professor of Contemporary Islamic Studies, University of Oxford

X + 146pp, paperback
UK £8.99 | US $16.00
ISBN 978-1-84774-011-3

OTHER TITLES FROM
KUBE PUBLISHING

Available online and from all good bookstores

Abu Hanifah: His Life, Legal Method and Legacy | A.K. Nadwi
UK £8.99 | US $13.50

A Journey through Islamic History | Y. Hashim and M. Begg
UK £14.99 | US $22.95

A Princess's Pilgrimage | Nawab Sikander Begum | UK £12.99

Against Smoking: An Ottoman Manifesto | A. Al-Aqhisari
UK £8.99 | US $16.00

British Secularism and Religion | Y. Birt, D. Husain and A. Siddiqui eds.
UK £7.99

Daily Wisdom: Selections from the Holy Qur'an | A.R. Kidwai
UK £10.99 | US $18.00

Daily Wisdom: Sayings of the Prophet Muhammad | A.R. Kidwai
UK £10.99 | US $18.00

Discover the Best in You! Life Coaching for Muslims | Sayeda Habib
UK £8.99 | US $14.95

Discovering the Ottomans | Ilber Ortayli | UK £9.99 | US $16.50

Gaza: Stay Human | Vittorio Arrigoni | UK £6.99 | US $12.95

Heavenly Bites: The Best of Muslim Home Cooking | K. Dawood
UK £9.99 | US $18.00

Imam Al-Ghazali: A Concise Life | Edoardo Albert | UK £6.99 | US $14.95

Islam in Victorian Britain: The Live and Times of Abdullah Quilliam
Ron Geaves | UK £16.99

The Muslim 100 | M.M. Khan | UK £19.99 | US $24.95

The War Within Our Hearts | H. Quadri and S. Quadri
UK £7.99 | US $11.95

Wandering Lonely in a Crowd: Reflections on the Muslim Condition in
the West | S.M. Atif Imtiaz | UK £9.99 | US $15.00